Slate

Slate

VOLUME ONE

Aenea Kanaan

RESOURCE *Publications* • Eugene, Oregon

SLATE
Volume 1

Copyright © 2026 Aenea Kanaan. All rights reserved. Except for brief quotations in critical publications or reviews, no part of this book may be reproduced in any manner without prior written permission from the publisher. Write: Permissions, Wipf and Stock Publishers, 199 W. 8th Ave., Suite 3, Eugene, OR 97401.

Resource Publications
An Imprint of Wipf and Stock Publishers
199 W. 8th Ave., Suite 3
Eugene, OR 97401

www.wipfandstock.com

PAPERBACK ISBN: 979-8-3852-7117-7
HARDCOVER ISBN: 979-8-3852-7118-4
EBOOK ISBN: 979-8-3852-7119-1

for little me, who dared to dream.

"I spent that summer as I had every summer before, racing through the forest behind my house down the path my father called the old logging road to a meadow thick with raspberry bushes whose thorns were my very first heroes because they did nothing with their life but protect what was sweet."
—ANDREA GIBSON, *Homesick: A Plea For Our Planet*

poetry gives us permission to feel deeply

i'm more than weary
for this world is not kind
to my mind or body

slate: volume one

a constant coexistence
between being the surveyor
and the surveyed
the performance is
always on

aenea kanaan

i'm sorry
i don't mean it
i can be careless with my words
with the ones who mean the world to me
why am i pushing away
those closest
i can't keep doing this
soon you'll have enough of this
and i know you don't deserve it
my energy is misplaced
i won't let your love go to waste
and if i hesitate
i'm sorry
i'm just hoping
there's no one you could think of
taking my place
it's silly to say it
i'm in my head that's what it is
pull myself out this time
oh why is it so hard to love,
and so easy to hide?
say it soft
stay soft
can't let my heart go cold

slate: volume one

and in my life i feel alive
100 miles and down to ride
free my mind

aenea kanaan

intimidated by my presence
diminishing myself
to make others comfortable
i know myself, i know my light
i do not seek to make you small
only to make you bright

slate: volume one

in the process of undoing

aenea kanaan

my being is not something i have to apologize for.

constantly in my head
overthinking how others perceive me
at every second
it's exhausting
being this aware
can't i relax?
sit back and relish the presence of this moment?
or am i condemned to remain
in the prison that has been my mind
sixty percent of the time
i want to feel free
i want to feel safe enough to give in
and let go
is it something i did wrong
or is this what society planned all along?
to bait me into believing that i could be enough
for something that won't stop taking
a system that is bent
on my back breaking
if this isn't my fault
why is it so hard to unlearn?
so hard to heal?
and so easy to return
to these snares and traps
that once sweet, have turned sour
on my tongue
now that i see what it was always destined to become
so why can't i stop beating myself up?
questioning and doubting my own presence
shrinking my light to make others comfortable
giving away the power i hold,
the power we all hold.
i'm not sure if you understand me
i'm not sure what that even means

aenea kanaan

it's too easy to run
and for what?
when all i want is to be seen.

slate: volume one

if i could
i would send a message to the manufacturer of my mind
a return to sender
after all this time
i would tell them i wish i wrote sooner
that this was a bit trickier than i expected
working this thing of mine
i'd ask if my spirit has a purpose
the way the trees stay rooted in the soil
rooted in themselves
while cleaning the air for all of us to breathe
without thanks or bare recognition
of the power they wield
is that light inside me too?

aenea kanaan

lately it's hard to breathe
especially in my heart
the cage of my ribs is shut tight
my wings won't open
i can't take flight
i feel tethered, not rooted,
to the ground

i feel upset at myself
it's one snowball effect of self doubt
and it leaves me hollow
at war with myself
when all i want is peace
why can't i practice what i preach
i wish it was that easy
they all say just stop doubting and start believing
i'm tired of pretending
i'm tired of leaving
if only it wasn't so easy

aenea kanaan

i wish a summer night would sweep me up
and take me under those wings of dusk
into the great beyond
the air feels warm and lovely on bare skin
in a forest that never sleeps
fireflies dance near the treetops
the sea is close by
salt stings the air and sings of the moon and her tides
but she never forgot the sun
as they met on the horizon
and she kissed him goodnight

slate: volume one

feeling it
embracing it
simply noticing it's there

aenea kanaan

exercise is a time where i feel most still,
most centered in my body

slate: volume one

i don't feel like i can simply exist

aenea kanaan

why do you need to take light to feel good?

slate: volume one

know me when i am big
star self see it all
even when i touch the ground
stay centered as i fall
but know i can't touch you now
and i see me, see i'm small

aenea kanaan

float me away
on soft clouds and sky
dappled in sunshine on an afternoon ride
time is irrelevant
when we're here together
losing hours in your eyes
your presence is just so heaven sent
like a reverie
melting into your arms like a bubble bath
it's decadent and lovely
i want to stay here always

where energy goes
your focus flows
where your focus goes
energy flows

aenea kanaan

when i'm at the bottom
of the barrel
and nothing is filling me up
i'm still just waiting
for that feeling
like walking on air
lift me up
hold my hands
and just lift me out
of the sunken place
lost in my mind
lost time
but you found me
again

sitting still in this moment
wondering if it's the only one
i'll have
one serene second
lost in the moment
freedom of mind
the way i used to pass the time
days felt like lifetimes
adventures were my pastime
i still had time
to watch the setting sun
holding golden
slowly slipping under the horizon
flashes prick the night
like little stars that light the hills
a world has just woken up
my feet touch the ground
safe in the soul of the soil
i'm loose in the night
free, i'm unbound
i'll fly back to you
when the ocean clouds wash me to shore
on tides of silky rose
and i rise, glistening
to sink into your peace
once more

aenea kanaan

but you can't comprehend it
you just couldn't contemplate
what it takes
to feel safe and sound
in this body

slate: volume one

my belonging rests with me now.

aenea kanaan

am i asking too much?am i too much?
~no, you're never too much
you are always enough.

<growing pains>
this relationship has made me so much more aware of my trauma and how it's still affecting me. it's actively forced me to see myself and go through the uncomfortable feeling of being exposed and vulnerable to someone i cherish so much. you never want someone to see you like that, but there's something liberating about being so open, and not moving to hide from you. it's scary, it's not always easy or fun. but i believe this is truly real, something that pushes both of us to learn more about ourselves and grow more deeply than ever before, to evolve into our higher selves together. this must be what it means to grow with someone. something i've yearned for, yet secretly feared.

aenea kanaan

down and out in my head

i'm just not sure
what to say
anymore
maybe i should say nothing
might be better than something
better than feeling
like i'm too much to deal with
it's sad i feel this small
i've dug this hole
and i don't know how
to get out of these walls
stuck
in a pitfall of my own creation

aenea kanaan

take me to a sunlit grove
forget about everything
it's all a daydream
in this sunset cove

you don't like when i'm selfish
but i can't help it
when i look at you
there's nothing i wouldn't do
to stay by your side
i'm along for ride
i'll be your baby
i'll be your everything
just let me keep you
all to myself
you don't like when i'm selfish
when i'm around you
i'm glowing
i just can't help
my feelings showing
there's nothing fake about it
selfish
i can't help it
you like it

aenea kanaan

i have so much love in my heart for you
i cherish you
deeply
i'll keep you safe
endlessly
no need to question me
protect that energy
just focus on me
i'll show you the way

slate: volume one

my essence is gold
the root of my being
my deep down soul
my aura gold, or
a really pretty purple blue,
like a periwinkle hue

aenea kanaan

it's crazy how just when you think
you've felt it all
you can feel
so.much.more.
hold you so close now
cuz i'm scared to lose it all

sometimes the hardest thing to do
is to stay right here
i want to flinch
i want to turn away
i want to run and hide
all of those parts of me
i don't want to let you inside
i wish i was easy
to let you see me

aenea kanaan

a journey to self /
/ finding you again

stay stuck,
or grow?
it's my body
my own
in my head
i'm thrown
these waves are pounding
harder and harder
on top of my head
and i just want
to see you again
i wake up
buried in sand
know you need me
lost in this foreign land
i'll pray to a light
to guide me home
i'll pray,
my head
in my hands
see me
fallen and lone
my wings beat
to fly me
heart beats
to guide me
see you in the twilight
when i come home
i touch down
on pine tree tops
and run to see you
but deep down,
i'm scared you left already
on those night wings

aenea kanaan

you could have just left
but now i see you
a branch above
sitting so gently
i missed you
you meet me
your touch is just heavenly
a roost in your arms

i never grow tired of loving you
in fact
my love for you
blooms like wild poppies
across the moors of my mind
it only grows stronger and deeper
over passing time
akin to wise sequoia trees
and their mighty roots miles down
grounded in the peace you've planted here
the peace we cultivate
together

aenea kanaan

i wish to be respected above all else

sitting in this sterile room
waiting to confront fear itself
[wisdom teeth]

aenea kanaan

making time for the still
is so important in a society
that can't stand still
make space for your thoughts
touch the infinite capacity of your emotions
and you can feel your essence
making space for yourself
makes space for those unheard
pushed aside and disregarded
by a society that cares too much
for plowing on and too little
for meeting people where they are

to be just as we are
lean into uncomfortable feelings
and you lean into yourself
just as you are
lean into the *bodhicitta*- our wounded, softened heart
the love that will not die
gentle and warm,
the awakened heart
holds you tight
reminds you,
you deserve your own compassion
it waits patiently for you.

aenea kanaan

talk is cheap
but it shouldn't be

we want it to be easy
because they make it seem so easy
but that's not the point is it
the point is so straightforward, so simple
that people don't realize that's it
it's not supposed to be easy
it's not supposed to be comfortable
it's not supposed to be certain
but of course, we want it to be
everyone is going through it
but we all play pretend
like that's not how it is
like that's not life
we want to believe the dream that was sold to us
when we were little
the one that fronted
that told us if we just tried hard enough
we could be happy and safe forever
and if we're not,
we didn't try hard enough
there must be something wrong
with us
we wanted it to feel
like how we knew it was always supposed to feel
so what then
when it doesn't?
what then
when you're not even sure what you're supposed to be feeling in the first place?
what then when it's nothing like you imagined?
perhaps you're feeling it alright,
and this is just how it's supposed to be
then why do i feel so off,
so confused,

aenea kanaan

like there's something wrong with me?
we're all just thrown here
into existing
and told to make something of it
i find loves and likes and the things that make me feel
and then we're told to make a living, 'keep it real'
when all i want is to keep feeling
to keep loving
without socially constructed worries running my mind
working for a paycheck, just to fill the time
time i could be using to live
like i'm supposed to.

don't think the worst
cuz the worst isn't true

aenea kanaan

the oak forest's trees reached their sprawling, twisted branches towards the sky, looking stark and ominous in the dark, especially compared to the pines. their dark was a different kind, comforting to her. when night fell there, she felt safe wrapped in the blanket of navy under their soft feathery branches. held by those silent guardians of the night.

i'm not just a body
you get to use up
my autonomy
has been robbed from me
my kindness taken advantage of
again and again
but i have stolen back
what was always mine.

aenea kanaan

it's not that i don't know you
i just had a very different version of you
that existed in my head
a dream of who i hoped you could be
but i've found they don't line up
when i see you clearly

slate: volume one

a passenger in your feelings

aenea kanaan

the light in me honors the light in you.
[lightwise]

rain
wash it all away
take the fear and take the pain
until there's nothing left to say

aenea kanaan

it's not up to you
to navigate someone else's emotions

the incomparable power
of a soul that is untarnished and whole
of one who holds their own

aenea kanaan

you're scared it'll
make
you
feel
open up
if you truly want
the real
(most people don't)

slate: volume one

we've forgotten our place in the ecosystem of the world
as humble stewards, not all consuming dictators.

aenea kanaan

i feel like water
i feel it rising
flushing my cheeks
everything comes to the surface
so easily
show my colors
spill into the room
slide down my face like tears
no tryna hide it
i'm dying
inside
tides rise and swell
dragged back to the depths
into all the feelings i don't need
everything i don't want to tell
powerfully embodied
do you see it, crashing within me?

too many worries anxieties doubts and fears
about the future
take up space
my fear of losing everything and everyone i love
my lack of faith in the future
breathe into myself
this is all i have
nurturing what you need
in this moment
today
forced routines and rituals
become dull vices
when you don't reach
the deepest parts of you unseen
and give them the love they need
whatever that looks like
today

aenea kanaan

sometimes
i get so stuck in routine
i forget what i need

i know that's how it happens
but it doesn't mean it isn't
fucking sad.

aenea kanaan

she is an immensely caring, thoughtful and inspiring person
she would give her left arm if i so much as suggested i was in
need of one
i've never seen someone put others first so much that sometimes
it hurts
because i want her to prioritize her
her selflessness is quite unmatched by anyone else i know
this is obviously a good problem to have
but please don't forget to water yourself too
[mama]

slate: volume one

i am constantly reminded of what really matters

aenea kanaan

the sauna has been a place
of safety and healing
where i first started
to take up space
heal me, body and soul
heal, my body

i don't feel at home here
these people
i've been trying in vain
to convince myself
that i feel comfortable around
realizing my inner voice
was gagged and bound

aenea kanaan

oh the ocean is
oh so old
old but gold
glitz and glamour
old school grandeur
in the marine

call me santa claus
the way i gift my presence

aenea kanaan

the summer is back
and i'm alive again

standing still
i can finally see the sky
uninterrupted for once

aenea kanaan

you got me good
i'll admit
i got it bad

slate: volume one

sleepy bear dunes, never sleeping on you

aenea kanaan

i'm in a period of my life where i'm acknowledging all the things that don't feel right for me and releasing them. this baggage can't come with me where i'm headed.

we are inherently pure
but lack of love
causes distortion and chaos

aenea kanaan

i have a hole in my heart where these connections should be and it aches within me

and i know
i have done love
i feel complete

aenea kanaan

feels like my autonomy
has been stripped away from me
my authenticity gone with the wind
so much for all that
as long as you're in the driver's seat
so much for your ideas
but don't worry, they say
you can trust us
you can trust that we know you
better than you know yourself
/system/programming/control/

shaking
never felt this numb
to the tips of my toes
oh it hurts
i want it to go
i never thought it would come to this
would feel like this
oh i feel so low
i'm empty
speechless
you got me good
in the worst way

aenea kanaan

so alone
curled up
with all my woes

how powerful,
to be united through
what we love
rather than
what we hate.
[new friends]

aenea kanaan

there are *also* forces of good in this world

what every man should know about a woman:
how to make her feel loved
safe, and whole
to quiet a mind of doubts
from baggage he never packed,
but carries nonetheless
to be there when she needs him
to show up,
to really be there
dependable, solid and steadfast
so his love for her is
a grounded unmovable force
no matter what wave swells into shore
no matter how big
they're protected
secure in their bubble
held as we
free to be you and me
to know i can roam
but at the end of the night
you'll always hold out your arms
and welcome me home

thank you for loving me as a whole person. thank you for loving me, even when it's difficult. thank you for showing me that the true power of love isn't just being there when it's easy and fun, but for when it's not. thank you for showing me the true capacity of what it means to love someone fully, every single day. thank you for showing me that even when i feel at my worst, my lowest, my most vulnerable, that i'm just as lovable.
i've never had someone show me love like this. love that doesn't leave, love that isn't dependent, love that doesn't feel conditional, love i don't have to earn. love that will still be there after a bad day. love that lights up my inner child with laughter and play.
love that makes me feel seen in the rawest way.
love that tucks me in at night and meets me in my dreams.
it can be hard to give love, but i've realized the hardest thing for me is actually receiving it.
feeling unconditionally lovable wasn't something i knew until knowing you.
you've shown me that it's not asking for a lot and i deserve every bit of it.
thank you,
i love you.

slate: volume one

the art of slowness

aenea kanaan

goodnight love, goodnight light
goodnight guardians
of the night

slate: volume one

stop giving them room in your head.
[evict them.]

aenea kanaan

we forget that we are fluid, not fixed
we ebb and flow like the tides
emotions shift like the weather
we are not bound to one moment
we are capable of change
we are flexible
if we allow ourselves
to move with the energy
of the universe
moving all around us
shifting grains of sand
we are part of the cosmic dance

everything is too much
i can't breathe
i'm drowning
this society is a disease
it consumes until there's nothing more
nothing left
we're the ones set as bait
we're the heave we're the heft
to keep it running best
i feel like a caged animal
it's breaking me
they're trying to
break
me
in
don't feel like myself
i'm slipping away
don't really laugh these days
it's too hard to
hold it all together
keep everything in line
one big blow
and they all fall down
i want to let go

aenea kanaan

i find my soul
in the golden hour
touch is soft
like peony petals
and morning dew

slate: volume one

how i would love a seaside siesta~

aenea kanaan

breathe slow
and i remember
when light bathed me
in a golden glow
and held me there
still as snow

slate: volume one

know you are a divinely protected soul

aenea kanaan

my heart feels lonely
at this little outdoor concert
in a sunlit moment under the trees
at a tiki bar
and i can't believe how much i miss you
doesn't feel the same without you here
waiting on you
my other half
i need you here
if only you were
we could get cocktails
at the tiki bar
and giggle at our inside jokes
like idiots
having
so
much
fun

it feels like you take me for granted
you don't know much i mean to you
you think i'll always be here
you think i write poems for just anyone
you should feel special
i even open my heart to you like this
do i have to treat you like everyone else
to make you realize how much
i let you in?
(you're not reciprocating my energy)

aenea kanaan

drinking sake
feeling bubbly
lovely on my lips

world shattering conclusion: you gotta allow yourself to be seen to have connection

aenea kanaan

i feel like shit
feel unheard
i fucked it
let my trust issues get in the way
listened to my insecurities all day
stayed in my head
and pushed you away

may i be safe
may i be loving and kind to myself
may i trust myself and those i love
may i forgive myself
every step takes us closer to home
i wish to release the baggage i carry, it's heavy and it's weighing me down with all its doubts, fears, and insecurities. it's still really hard for me to trust. i thought simply being in a healthy relationship would fix that but i think there's more to it than that. everything i've said and done has stemmed from not feeling secure in the moment.
i wish to be secure, i wish to trust, i wish to open my heart.
i don't want to ruin something amazing because of things that happened to me in the past
this is something i will actively work towards, even though it's hard.

aenea kanaan

too much
not enough
hold up
just right
is it too much
to wanna be loved up
asking for it all
it's not that
you're not enough
i guess i was
just too much

i love you
for who you are
who you were
and who you'll become

aenea kanaan

this anxiety creeps
in the late night
and loves to pounce in the morning
i didn't realize how lonely
it would be
i miss it all so much
like damn
it's all new, it's all over
some things feel gone forever
i miss 'cuse, i miss you
i don't know where it goes from here
my path isn't so clear
anymore
is it written in the stars?

and i think heaven
smells like rain
lost in a trance
for a second
like when you call my name
suspended
in this moment in time

aenea kanaan

don't you know,
you gotta pay to play

i feel supremely misunderstood
i wish i was good
i feel so left out
but i'm sitting myself out

aenea kanaan

stomach in knots
right from the jump
as auburn light sneaks in
the morning is tainted
from this unease sinking
deeper into my torso
off the deep end
dropping like a stone
into my turbulent pool
dire like dark blue
the writings on the wall
i tried to play it cool but
can i really have it all?
have i played myself a fool
at last?
was this in the cards,
do i stand a chance?
i never imagined
growing up was this hard

some people are good
others are just good at hiding
i wear my heart on my sleeve
mean what i say
and speak what i believe
i just can't keep it down
my face like glass
and most don't like that

aenea kanaan

anchor light

slate: volume one

i want to walk on treetops

aenea kanaan

blue
emanating from you
i can see it in your eyes
feel the sadness like it's my own
i could cry
seeing you keep it inside
all on your own
you walk this road
miles away from home
feeling broken
like you can't keep going
if only you knew
if only you believed in you
because you're strong enough
that's good enough
maybe
it would be enough
to make you believe
you could make it through
they're watching you
angels above, all guarding you
wings wrapped round
i know you can't see
but you can't fall now
blue
like clear night skies
lights guide me
and they've got you too

i care for you deeply
i've been picky now
because others mistreat me
not like you
you're all sweet on me

aenea kanaan

don't ever feel bad for feeling you
it's okay to be blue
coming from a sad boy,
you're speaking my truth
truthfully i adore you
because you make me feel
my butterflies, you set them loose
i'm over the moon
oh to be a youth
i don't think it's because i'm young
that i fell this soon
you
your soul
it's like i know you
but you're all too new
twin flame you make my heart race
yet there's so much ease
being in this place
comfortable enough to let you see
letting you in my space
it's big for me
you're the same i know
finally reciprocity
mutual state of flow

trying to stop myself from sinking
i miss you so bad
it's all i'm thinking
i know it's different
and i'm happy for you
but part of me keeps wondering
where you flew
trying to keep myself from sinking
it'll all work out, i'm hoping
but it's hard to stop myself thinking

aenea kanaan

there's power in these poems
power in the words she wrote
your sword is sharp
my tongue is sharper
back against the wall
pinned with my pen at your throat
i smell the fear
feel your heartbeat,
fluttering out of control
waiting for the final blow
cowering
totally exposed
but maybe
just this time,
i won't
i'm a lover at heart
because the truth is all i need
it's enough to rip you apart

after rain
the air smells like
mist and fire

aenea kanaan

light and love
protects this space
light and love
guides my pace

shits getting to me
the nine to five
there's a reason everyone's anxious
it's making us sick
it's not hard to see
we're not meant for captivity
it feels like i'm pacing
a tiger in my too tiny cage
i know i chose to be here
but it still feels the same
just set me free
let me leave
this lifestyle is all consuming
it's eating me alive
my heart is heavy under all this weight
my legs feel like crumbling pillars
about to collapse
it doesn't feel right to put my body under
all this stress
for what?
for who?
certainly not me
i'm only here for a paycheck
my wellbeing is much deeper than money
it's gotten to the point
where a rest sounds like an oasis
and tastes like honey

aenea kanaan

it's hard to hold onto your own voice
through the noise
nothing is what it seems
this pressure feels insane

it's breaking my heart
to see you this way
i know it's not about me
but for you
i really feel that way
i see everything to love
and nothing to hate

aenea kanaan

that awful crushing feeling
when you realize you aren't anyone's best friend
and even though it's not intentional
it's the distance
why can't i be someone's favorite?

what if the sun
the moon
and the stars in the sky
gave it all up
to be just a little guy?
to walk on the ground,
the shell of the earth
only to look up at night
and wonder
about those distant, twinkling lights
way up high
what must it feel like
to have a place in the sky?

aenea kanaan

keep butting heads
over silly things
silly fights got us
both walking away hurting
meanwhile i'm here
dreaming up dates for us
wishing i could just see you
if it could be me and you
i'm only annoyed cuz i miss you
only upset because i'm
in too deep
and the space gets me feeling
it way too deep
idealistic as fuck
heart on my sleeve
i'm irritable only cuz i give a fuck
you're mad at me
meanwhile
i'm daydreaming about what
we
could be
can't stay mad at me
and i can't keep an attitude
i come back to you

it seems like sometimes
i only catch glimpses
of myself
when i used to see her
all the time

aenea kanaan

i wonder who paints the sky…

                                                give them a raise!

slate: volume one

midnight espresso
take a bow
goodnight moon
[*grey ghost, detroit*]

aenea kanaan

my parents moved away
and i don't know how to feel
i knew it was coming
but somehow it came too fast
and everyday i have to remind myself
it's real
the last root of my childhood
has left and taken flight
and now i don't know where
i belong
never realized how hard it is
to be the only one staying
when everyone else
is leaving
i'm pretty depressed
i can't even lie
i miss being a kid
all the good times are flooding back
in my mind's eye

your love in a cup
peppermint for my throat
open my chest
under the weather
sick making me soft
feeling that soft feminine
i'm delicate too
just because i'm strong
doesn't mean i don't need care too

aenea kanaan

got my soup,
got my man
i'm ready to go,
to any land.

we shouldn't have to fight for our peace
our birthright is sovereignty
this world profits off us
living in a state of fear

aenea kanaan

on the shore
rippled sunlight in the waves
dancing on the crests
like little amber jewels
dregs from the deep
pulsing beating hearts of light
sunbeam, copper and black tea
we come from the deep
but return to the sky
made of earth, wind and sea
filled with the energy
of a thousand tiny suns
it lives on in us
the spark that keeps
the fire in our eyes lit

isn't it crazy
how life is more about
how it *feels*
than how it looks
or actually is
it's all about
~*the fantasy*

aenea kanaan

feel how you feel (or don't feel)

i feel like no one understands
how i'm really feeling
and if i'm being honest,
they definitely don't.
how could they?
it's starting to feel like
it's just me
the truth is
i don't know how i feel
about a lot of things anymore
i don't have that urge to have kids
i don't even know what i'd do with a niece
i feel so much
but with this
i feel almost nothing at all
i can't force how i feel
and part of me wishes i could
because i just don't have the same wants
and it's lonelier than ever here
i don't feel like anyone around me
truly understands
and i'm so closed off,
i don't even want to give them a chance
the grey outside mirrors
the grey in my mind
it's foggy in here
i'm not sure how i feel,
it's all starting to look unclear
things don't feel the same
glasses of feelings are pouring from the ceiling
i'm drenched, i'm shaking
it's all mixed and i can't see a thing
not the fun kind of showers
i'm cold and alone

aenea kanaan

in the night hours
thinking these thoughts
i could keep you up at night
my heart's just not in it

i'm tired of feeling alone
is it pathetic
that i write about it
all the time?

aenea kanaan

a lonely ghost in a loud room
i'm trying but i just can't hear you
i wish you would
take
me
home

what hurts most
is losing the you
i thought i knew
the one i love so dearly
who always made me smile
i miss him so much
it's killing me
what if this is the end
we both need a break
but i don't want the story to be done
a million thoughts in my head
but i won't press send
i didn't want to close the book this early
i thought it would be a series
at least a trilogy
it's just not the same
right now
my energy is drained
and i'm not sure how
to keep going like this
something's got to give
and i can't give anymore

aenea kanaan

i'm crushed
my scorpio emotions might be
too intense for you
the depths are overwhelming
even for me

pondering existence
under the pines
up on this hilltop
my little smoke stop
for the night
with novie
we are the castles' stoic watchmen
on our lookout hill
keeping watch over the neighborhood
within willow kingdom walls
trees of peace
swaying gently in the breeze
on this cold december evening
with a sky like slate
rolling and drifting like the sea
my hands are cold and numb now
i've never seen the clouds move
so quickly
making the journey back
is never as bad as alone
glad to have my trusty steed
and lights to guide us home
i taste like mango sherbet
and your arms feel like haven

aenea kanaan

I CHOOSE LOVE

it's nice to feel safe
loved and heard
safe inside these walls
held and warm
grateful for my lights
thankful for this man
you really keep me calm
i've never known peace
like you
beautiful golds and pink hues
you hold me down
into the ground
deep and true

aenea kanaan

all is said and done
truth has come out
it's only clarity now
i don't feel anger's heat
just sweet relief
like the calm after the storm
when the air is quiet
and the waters warm
i feel nothing but peace
knowing in my hands
i'll never come to harm
because my words won't sting like yours
and i deserve so much more
you never made me feel good
in fact
your words really hurt
and shaped the way i saw myself
it's the way i shrink
pull into my sleeves
and let you make me feel
so small
i know now, that's not love
even now you say the same things
so casually
like they didn't make me cry
when i'm alone
words that tear me down
and put me on the spot
not in the fun way
but you don't see
because i don't let you in
anymore
you've shown me that you won't change
you don't know the weight of your words

and you can't take criticism
you poke at my insecurities
but are so quick to get butthurt
when the tables are turned
how funny it is
that you don't want to get burned
but you're an unassuming pit of embers
the fun is over the fire's out
but the cinders burn
in the spots that hurt
too raw and too fresh
for any heat
but you can't catch the blame
because it's not intentional?
because it's 'just a joke'?
fuck that.

aenea kanaan

simply existing again

i swear i saw darkness fall
as lush and rich
as a ripe blackberry

aenea kanaan

when every day is full of love
[a life worth living]

so why does it have to be so difficult?
i don't want to lose you
my love for you spans trenches
oh i'm feeling alive now
i want to be wanted
i want to feel it so palpably
it's indistinguishable
from anything else but the real thing
i don't want to question everything
i need to know
you want me
down to my soul
to my bones
there's someone who can give that to me
and i thought it was you
can't you?

aenea kanaan

i've got all my eggs in your basket, one might say.

slate: volume one

everything really does get better when you start surrendering and open yourself to love

aenea kanaan

what happens when you're no longer of use?
(to them)

he's just a kid
who's raised himself

aenea kanaan

tell me we'll find something like home some day. you're the only thing that feels close to it now.

i'm too sensitive? too dramatic?
or are you simply
uncomfortable
with emotional expression?

aenea kanaan

time to put the thoughts down
and let your brain relax

big dipper
bigger up close, way up in the sky
floating over darkness
above a comforter of feather white clouds
they keep the lights beneath warm
at a glance
it could be the sea
it's amazing people really think the earth is flat
the constellations are tilted up here,
imprinted on a semicircle of dusk
nothing is flat
not even that ass
i'm mesmerized
i wish they could black out the plane
and make it a planetarium,
just for the night
so i could drink it all in
just for the flight

aenea kanaan

i had to write it down
it's too beautiful
i always do
on solo trips

my tides rise
cheeks flush
wrapped in heat
hot to the touch
i'm antsy
ready to fly
hard to sit still
with this fire on my skin
and a tsunami within
feeling turbulent
with nothing to cool me down
rain
where are you now?
these clouds look ready to break
grey swirling mist
a frosty mountain range
ready to pour

aenea kanaan

a duffel bag on wednesdays
/child of divorce\

slate: volume one

the seeker
on the search for truth
it can't stay buried forever

aenea kanaan

i get really lost in you
the way we move

unflinching
unwavering
straight in the eyes
right to the soul
i won't cover mine

aenea kanaan

what color are the sparkles
behind your eyes?
~purple blue like cobalt diamonds

slate: volume one

what do you want to accomplish in this life?
what do i *really* want?
to be an inspiration for good
to give others permission to be themselves
to liberate the universe
to embody love.

aenea kanaan

not if,
but when.
(a reminder)

love is the only thing
that really matters
everything else
dissolves away
in its presence

aenea kanaan

like just what do you say
to somebody
who 'unintentionally' gave you
so much trauma?

isn't it sweet
isn't it lovely
i've never felt secure around you
lights out
and i'm really scared now
you left me for the ghosts and ghouls
laughing all the way
still afraid of the dark
i wonder who's to blame

aenea kanaan

the earth feels like home
she'll treat you divine
as one of her own
if you revere and protect her

slate: volume one

black cat poetry
shamus and oak street
a haunted old house

aenea kanaan

and the pieces did, indeed, start falling back into place.

people feel like they can
be themselves around me
but where do i feel comfortable?
i just wanna be secure
i'm always in between
this space is exhausting
i just want it to feel like home
again
but it's never the same again

aenea kanaan

crying like every other day
for a while now
time keeps feeling like it's flying
just can't keep the blues away
profoundly lost in thought
i just want to feel better
can't it be better
maybe it's worth it
how lovely it is to think
there's some grand meaning
an ultimate scheme to justify
my pretty little fears
it's all for the character development
it's just a couple thousand tears

slate: volume one

sadness and slate

aenea kanaan

you're my heart, you have mine forever.

it's quite
heartbreaking
not being able to help
the one you love
oh please
let me lift you up,
you're sinking.
please please
stand up
you can touch,
i promise.

aenea kanaan

be here.

i'm head over heels for you
i just want the best for us
i see us whole and healed
just trust
i choose me
i choose you
i choose us
i'm weary of living in fear
ungrounded
unbalanced
not here
i choose to live with love
in my heart
and light on my mind
with you,
by my side
we can get through
anytime

aenea kanaan

there are moments when it is necessary to restrict the amount of
people who have access to your mind.
you have power over your inner world. if they're not here for your
highest good,
don't let them in.

warm with the rising air
the ice started to loosen
dripping then cascading
until the forest
was raining
gone like it's a different day
just an hour later
faded mist, like a dream

aenea kanaan

point is,
you aren't safe to me.

this soup feels really special
and it's all for me
i'm eating my love
it's savory and satisfying,
how you say
~*umami.*

aenea kanaan

i can't lie
it's hard for me to feel rejected
it's hard for everyone, i know
but i take it a bit too personally than most
it's something i work on
but it can feel like rejection, cold and hard
dismissal, apathy, like they don't care enough about you
not true
at the root
it's really not about you
some people can't accept help
are too ashamed or self-loathing to accept
a small kindness
a gift, perhaps
it isn't that you're giving too much
or that there's something wrong
with what you *can* give
sometimes i wish
you could stop pushing me away
and let me help you
please let me stay
i'm not your enemy
please, i'm your friend.

great blue heron
oh how wise you are
bringing me new headspace
on those slate wings
grateful
for how you sweep up
all the things i need to let go
and release them into the sky

aenea kanaan

as much as you love red,
you're blue.

even as a nomad on this earth
i still need somewhere to call home
just one place
that feels like my own
i think even the farthest wanderer
the most inspired vagabond,
must need somewhere
to call their lair

aenea kanaan

an avalanche of light

on those souls with no tether to their own,
watch carefully and protect your energy.
you can always shield from more hurt,
but you cannot change them
an authentic individual
on the other hand
speaks truth to power
secure in myself because
it comes from within
living in congruence
with who i am
down to my bones
the narcissist slayer
your game doesn't work on me
anymore
i see to your core
just like you suspected
and i refuse to bend
how unsettling
i've pulled your plug
now you're spluttering out
like an old car that
just
won't
start.

aenea kanaan

i'm a truth seeker
a healer, an alchemist
on a quest to spread light
a true intellect with a soul
from the stars
a basketball player
and a god damn
demon slayer.

slate: volume one

yes, i dare!

aenea kanaan

but you,
you make me feel less alone.
seen by my rock,
the unsung hero.

sick of waiting up for you
…so i won't

aenea kanaan

this video game gets pretty fun once you learn how to play

breath like a swell
rising through my chest
moves with the current

aenea kanaan

slate grey silver linings
choose to see the glimmers

slate: volume one

in a kimono
in kyoto
[nihon nostalgia]

aenea kanaan

bonfire nights
stars in full sight
oh how i long for
these sweet summer flights

slate: volume one

sad boy writing poems
lover girl in my feelings
stay subtweeting
but not on twitter

aenea kanaan

i don't have a lot to say
your actions spoke loud enough
or inaction i should say
it's so ironic that i
was still the one to hit you up
after all those years
and you're still just the same
after all those tears
the first time was just heartbreak
but now i've lost you
the girl i knew
must have been from
a daydream instead
now i'm grieving the loss
of someone
i thought i knew
the death
of a person who was never true

so many of my self loving and healthy thoughts come from the
things you've said to me

aenea kanaan

whenever he's not around
i find myself subconsciously searching
for him
thinking i catch glimpses
but it's not him
yearning for the one i covet

god forbid i want someone to take care of me for once.

aenea kanaan

i thought i thought i thought
all i do is think!

two dollar wine
my favorite times

aenea kanaan

i will not be stuck, i refuse.
that's the type of feeling i rebuke.

no one ever held my heart
and then this one stuck
and now we're locked in

aenea kanaan

soft and gentle,
like the sun
warm and bright,
i miss your light
divine and blazing,
like the sun
untouchable yet capable
of being felt
nothing shines like you
the ultimate source of life
i'm beyond elated
to see you again

it takes a light
to know
a light

aenea kanaan

no matter how dark it gets,
i will always look for the beauty

slate: volume one

what does it mean
to be home?

aenea kanaan

i'm such a sucker for the good old days
how it used to be
when i didn't think it would change
it's always so hard for me
when nothing stays the same

those clouds.
i've never seen the sky look more
like an ocean
[a poem i wrote, after the storm]

aenea kanaan

hello,
libra moon
look at you
all scooby doo
nested in those fluffy clouds
like a cartoon
within seconds
you've popped out all on your own
suddenly so grown
the sky is smoke and mirrors
the moon, an easter egg
shielded by a shimmering veil
mist in the night
spring frogs sing,
spinning tales of great height

who would have thought
it would be me and you,
you and i here
in this place,
together.
who would have known
how much you would mean
to me
from a secret crush to known
from girlhood to grown
well i'll let you know,
it was a real pleasant surprise.

aenea kanaan

cleanse my spirit,
cleanse my tides
help me let go
of whatever resides
until all that's left
is love

slate: volume one

soft, but shielded.

aenea kanaan

the birds don't care
the sky is gray
for the treetops
still
dance and sway
they'll still come out
to play

sometimes
i think past and present moments
connect
and create a new meaning
from lonely to held
like hearing the same song
from a time on your own
to now surrounded by people
you feel safe around
the association shifts,
and it chooses love instead.

aenea kanaan

the sun feels golden warm
honey sinking into my skin
i drink it in
i missed you more

feeling really at home here
right above my heart
warm,
my light spills around me
glows uncontrollably now
i just have to let it out
i don't really care
what you think
it's almost unbelievable.

aenea kanaan

i am the wind,
i am the sea
i am the sunshine,
and the trees

you
like an arrow,
straight and true.
you give me the truth,
even if it stings like salt.
rather have that,
than all glitter and gold
but nothing to hold.
some people talk like wind.
one moment it's a gale
the next,
it's like nothing has been.
gone,
with the wind
at least you're a straight shooter.

aenea kanaan

whatever i touch
turns
to gold

slate: volume one

i love the trees that reach up
to the sky with
big, fluffy arms
that look more like silky seaweed
than needles
my favorite eastern pine

aenea kanaan

i've realized
it is okay
to lounge, to lay
to laze around and smell the flowers
to be caught in a moment of golden contrast
you don't always have to be
doing
going
all
day
long.
it is okay
to put your feet up and rest
you deserve to lounge in the sun
and drink in the dew
let your eyes rest
and soak in warmth.

slate: volume one

oh how i love to lay

aenea kanaan

once he finds his power again
he'll be golden

do you think the birds ever get tired of flying?
do they ever want to sleep in,
curl up and go to bed?
what does it mean to be a bird?
..to be one with the sky and the soar

aenea kanaan

there's something wild about him
and i really love it

slate: volume one

i encourage you to seek your peace.

www.ingramcontent.com/pod-product-compliance
Lightning Source LLC
Chambersburg PA
CBHW051047160426
43193CB00010B/1099